HOLLYWOOD WEDDINGS

EDITED BY J.C. SUARÈS

THOMASSON-GRANT

Published by Thomasson-Grant, Inc.

Copyright © 1994 J. C. Suarès.
Captions copyright © 1994 J. Spencer Beck.

Printed in Hong Kong.

ISBN 1-56566-059-5

00 99 98 97 96 95 94 5 4 3 2 1

Inquiries should be directed to:
Thomasson-Grant, Inc.
One Morton Drive, Suite 500
Charlottesville, Virginia 22903-6806
(804) 977-1780

Merle Oberon
WUTHERING HEIGHTS, 1939

*One of Hollywood's most mysterious beauties, the half-Indian
(a secret she kept from the public), Tasmanian-born one-time London
café hostess called Queenie O'Brien made an exotically lovely—
if tragic—bride in the achingly romantic Samuel Goldwyn classic.
As regal and elusive as the character she played in that film,
Oberon married a succession of powerful men in real life,
eventually settling into jet-set retirement in Acapulco, Mexico
(a town she helped put on the map), with her third husband,
Italian industrialist Bruno Pagliai, whom she later divorced
to marry much-younger actor Robert Wolders.*

{veryone loves a wedding. And no one loves a wedding more than Hollywood. From the silver screen of the silent era to the video screen of today, some of the world's most memorable stars have been joined in holy matrimony on the studio backlot.

Although there are many films (*A Wedding, Royal Wedding, Quiet Wedding, The Member of the Wedding,* to name a few) that revolve around the event itself, there are countless other, more endearing pictures, which feature wedding scenes that will forever be remembered fondly by anyone who has ever marched down the aisle or someday hopes to.

Just as no two brides are alike, neither are any two big-screen nuptials. There are lavish weddings (*Camelot, The Scarlet Empress*) and more domestic affairs (*Father of the Bride, Brigadoon*); macabre ceremonies (*The Bride of Frankenstein, The Bride Wore Black*) and funny occasions (*Private Benjamin, The Heartbreak Kid*). Sometimes weddings begin a movie (*The Godfather*), and sometimes they end it (*The Palm Beach Story*). More often than not, the ceremony is interrupted (*The Philadelphia Story, The Graduate*); and occasionally the wedding never takes place at all (*The Bride Wasn't Willing*)!

If the drama and romance of these celluloid celebrations aren't enough, Hollywood's real-life weddings blur the distinction between reality and fantasy. Is it Joan Crawford the woman or Joan Crawford the actress who takes her vows with future husband Douglas Fairbanks, Jr. in *Our Modern Maidens?* Was seventeen-year-old Elizabeth Taylor's first marriage to hotel heir Nicky Hilton just a publicity ploy for her upcoming picture, *Father of the Bride?* And did Ava Gardner *really* marry Mickey Rooney, after all?

Although the off-screen marriages rarely lasted as long as the on-screen ones, these lavish, sometimes sentimental, but always glamorous affairs catered to our sublimest fantasies. Featuring gowns by Edith Head or Jean-Louis and often financed by the likes of Mr. Mayer himself, how could they not? And if Elizabeth Taylor, Tinseltown's most famous real-life and *reel*-life bride, is no longer the blushing virgin she was when she first walked down the aisle escorted by Spencer Tracy over forty years ago, she is still a star who marries for love each and every time as convincingly as the first.

Corinne Griffith
THE LADY IN ERMINE, 1927 (RIGHT)
*Billed as "the world's most beautiful woman" long before
Hedy Lamarr captured that title, Hollywood's "Orchid Lady"
graced over forty silent films in just fifteen years before retiring
from movies in her thirties a wealthy woman. The splendor of the
scene here, where the thrice-married, convent-educated actress
glides down the aisle in a sumptuous silk taffeta-and-feathers gown
between two columns of dashingly uniformed soldiers, is a heady
reminder of the days when stars <u>and</u> pictures were still big.*

Natalie Wood
INSIDE DAISY CLOVER, 1965 (OVERLEAF, LEFT)
*A child star like Elizabeth Taylor, the pretty, pint-sized daughter
of a Russian architect and a French ballerina (Wood could do a proper
plié before she could barely walk) makes a particularly poised bride
in a gown designed by Hollywood's premier costumer, Edith Head,
in this sometimes-hilarious Warner Bros. spoof on A Star Is Born.
Still smoking from her burnt-out real-life love affair with
Warren Beatty, the former Natasha Gurdin remarried
husband number one, Robert Wagner, in 1972.*

Elizabeth Taylor
FATHER OF THE BRIDE, 1950 (OVERLEAF, RIGHT)
*Was there ever a more beautiful bride than Elizabeth Taylor—
and she should know! Beginning with her publicity-propelled
marriage to hotel scion Nicky Hilton (coinciding cleverly with her
on-camera walk-down-the-aisle with movie dad Spencer Tracy),
the seventeen-year-old violet-eyed MGM star took the plunge
seven more times (twice to true love Richard Burton),
titillating movie fans and the media for forty years with her
on-again, off-again marital adventures.*

Maude George (with Erich von Stroheim)
THE WEDDING MARCH, 1928 (ABOVE)
Forced by a sense of princely duty (and greed), a Viennese nobleman scorns
his low-born true love and marries instead one of the least attractive
brides ever to (dis)grace a Hollywood wedding set. Directed by the
megalomaniacal von Stroheim (who also stars), this perverse, overblown,
and over-budget epic of Imperial Austrian decadence made a star of
pretty ingenue Fay Wray as the jilted peasant girl but effectively ended
the directing career of von Stroheim, who parodied himself outrageously
over twenty years later as the director-turned-butler of faded
silent film star Norma Desmond in Sunset Boulevard.

Joan Crawford (with Douglas Fairbanks Jr.)
OUR MODERN MAIDENS, 1929 (RIGHT)
Not always the somber-faced, shoulder-padded glamour queen of
her later pictures, the former down-at-the-heels shop clerk and chorus
girl born Lucille LeSueur was one of the Jazz Age's most winsome
and energetic film stars. Fresh from her overnight success in
Our Dancing Daughters, *silent-baby Crawford captured her*
handsome Modern Maidens *costar on-screen as well as off,*
marrying the scion of Hollywood's royal family in a well-orchestrated,
real-life publicity event and eventually dumping him a few
years later as her film career at MGM soared into the '30s.

Jane Russell and Marilyn Monroe
(with Elliott Reid and Tommy Noonan)

GENTLEMEN PREFER BLONDES, 1953

Wisecracking brunette Russell and ditsy blonde Monroe both get their man in this garish, fun-loving Howard Hawks musical update of the popular 1920s Anita Loos Broadway hit. The men in this wicked social satire are merely foils for the gold-digging, diamond-seeking duo, who eventually parade down the aisle in their Travilla-designed wedding gowns only to discover that true love—not money—brings happiness (and that hair color has nothing to do with it).

Claudette Colbert and Mary Astor
(with Rudy Vallee and Joel McCrea)
THE PALM BEACH STORY, 1942
One of the most famous wedding scenes in Hollywood history
tops off this zany Preston Sturges gagfest that poked fun at the idle
rich and made 1942 audiences forget about the war. Featuring
the hilarious likes of J. D. Hackensacker III (Vallee), Princess
Centimillia (Astor), and the Weenie King, the fast-flying film of sex,
greed, and mistaken identity slows down only long enough for a happy
ending—a triple-treat marriage with enough spouses for everyone.

Norma Shearer (with Leslie Howard)
SMILIN' THROUGH, 1932

*Three generations of tragic complications follow the murder of a
beautiful Victorian bride on her wedding day in this
three-handkerchief MGM tearjerker. At the height of her popularity,
the $6,000-per-week First Lady of the Metro lot was the real-life
bride of MGM production chief and boy wonder Irving Thalberg,
who successfully guided her career in the transition from silents
to talkies. Six years after Thalberg died in 1936 and following
a string of badly chosen roles, Shearer married a ski instructor
twenty years her junior and retired from the screen forever.*

Katharine Hepburn (with James Stewart and Cary Grant)

THE PHILADELPHIA STORY, 1940

*One of Hollywood's few scandal-free stars, Kate the Great as the
spoiled Tracy Lord created a memorable wedding-day scandal in the
picture that reestablished her career just two years after the actress
was voted box-office poison. After toying with just about every man in
the film (especially Stewart), Hepburn eventually dumps her intended
(John Howard), making it to the altar in the nick of time to remarry
ex-husband Grant. A wry and masterful look at the idle rich, the
Hepburn-owned, MGM-produced adaptation of the Philip Barry
Broadway hit (in which Hepburn starred in the part written expressly
for her) was a huge box-office smash and a great true-life comeback
for Hollywood's most celebrated independent lady.*

Julia Roberts (with Dylan McDermott)

STEEL MAGNOLIAS, 1989

*In her first major starring role, the striking twenty-one-year-old
Oscar-nominated beauty (who would soon go on to become the biggest
female box-office star in the world) held her own as a determined
young bride playing opposite the seasoned likes of Shirley MacLaine,
Sally Field, Olympia Dukakis, and Dolly Parton. Later, when her
off-screen wedding plans to actor Kiefer Sutherland fell through,
Roberts took an extended hiatus, only to reemerge married
to singer Lyle Lovett and poised to retake Tinseltown by storm.*

Elizabeth Taylor (with Don Taylor)
FATHER OF THE BRIDE, 1950
With a set designed by the legendary art director Cedric Gibbons
and a wardrobe by Academy-Award-winning costumer
Walter Plunkett, the ceremony in everyone's favorite wedding flick
is pure Hollywood fantasy. And so was teen-age Taylor's real-life,
publicity-staged marriage at the same time to millionaire playboy
Nicky Hilton. The two divorced only a few months later.

Goldie Hawn (with Albert Brooks)

PRIVATE BENJAMIN, 1980

One of the daffiest movie brides of all time made an even daffier army recruit in this madcap, Oscar-nominated tribute to life, love, and the pursuit of a husband. When Jewish princess Hawn's second spouse (Brooks) dies of a heart attack on their wedding night, the real-life former go-go dancer and "Laugh-In" star (and future steady companion of actor Kurt Russell) joins the military, suffering various misadventures and almost getting booted, before finding true love and husband number three (the final wedding scene is even more hilarious than the first) by the end of the story . . . well, <u>almost</u>.

Bette Davis (with Glenn Ford)
A STOLEN LIFE, 1946 (ABOVE)

Marriage to the feisty actress with a capital "A" would be a trial by fire for Miss Davis's four real-life husbands as well as her stoic costar in this melodramatic remake of a 1938 British vehicle for Elisabeth Bergner. Playing twins—one good, one bad—who both want the same man, the bug-eyed Jezebel sashays through her scenes wreaking havoc all the way to the altar. Davis would reprise her evil-twin role almost twenty years later in the gothic Dead Ringer.

Katharine Hepburn (with Spencer Tracy)
WOMAN OF THE YEAR, 1942 (RIGHT)

The acclaimed actor (he holds the record for the most Best Actor Academy Award nominations) who would become everyone's favorite Father of the Bride eight years later was the groom himself in the first of nine films paired with his friendly combatant Hepburn (she holds the record for most Best Actress Oscars). Ironically never married in real life, the down-to-earth Tracy and aristocratic Hepburn had little in common—on-screen or off—except love.

Natalie Wood (with Richard Beymer)
WEST SIDE STORY, 1961
*Wood's character Maria may "feel pretty, oh so pretty" dressed as
a bride for this dream sequence from Hollywood's biggest box-office
musical of all time, but her wedding to Tony is not meant to be.
Yet another cinematic version of the "Romeo and Juliet" tale,*
West Side Story *packed in young audiences who wanted to pine
along with the star-crossed lovers, particularly the popular
twenty-three-year-old real-life lover of matinée idol Warren Beatty.*

Simonetta Stefanelli (with Al Pacino)
THE GODFATHER, 1972

*Ethereal and alluring, Al Pacino's Sicilian bride in the most famous
cinematic pulp epic since* Gone With the Wind *provides a striking
foil to the ugliness surrounding the Corleone family business.
So beautiful is the aptly-named Apollonia that when she is killed
by a Mafia car bomb intended for her husband, we understand
Pacino's decision to turn his back on the "family" and later marry
the decidedly non-Italian outsider Diane Keaton.*

Talia Shire (with Sylvester Stallone)
ROCKY II, 1979

A two-hour comic-strip sequel to the first Rocky, *the follow-up picture is most endearing as a love story between the Italian Stallion (a nickname the actor/director earned in his first movie, a soft-core porno flick) and his new bride Shire. When Adrian rouses herself from a post-natal coma to rally Stallone in his quest for the heavyweight title, the film becomes an old-fashioned Hollywood testament to the cliché that "behind every good man is a woman."*

Grace Kelly and Prince Rainier of Monaco, 1956

Life imitated art when the serenely beautiful twenty-seven-year-old patrician actress retired from films to become Her Serene Highness Princess Grace of Monaco in a highly-publicized ceremony attended by crowned heads and Hollywood royalty alike. The previous year, the daughter of the wealthy former Philadelphia bricklayer and champion oarsman had played an aristocratic girl groomed to marry a crown prince in The Swan, *the star's last picture. Although there were occasional attempts through the years to persuade the Oscar-winning actress to return to her film career (she had left Hollywood having made only eleven movies), Princess Grace seemed content in the end to have her delicate face adorn postage stamps instead of publicity stills.*

**Rita Hayworth and Dick Haymes, 1953 (above)
and Orson Welles, 1943 (right)**

*The erotic queen of Forties films, the glamorous star born
Margarita Cansino (she was a cousin of Ginger Rogers) irritated
her powerful Columbia Studios boss and Svengali Harry Cohn,
who tried to direct his hottest property's messy personal affairs.
Standing up Victor Mature to marry husband number two,
Orson Welles, in a quickie ceremony, Hayworth eventually abandoned
Hollywood (and Welles) to wed jet-set playboy Aly Khan, only to
return freshly divorced two years later and ready to wed
down-on-his-luck singer Haymes. Her career a shambles,
the unforgettable star of* Gilda *went on to marry one more time
(unsuccessfully) before finally calling it quits in the marriage game.*

Ava Gardner and Mickey Rooney, 1942

*The wedding of the sensuous, sloe-eyed MGM starlet to that studio's
pint-sized number one box-office draw was the biggest event the
sleepy farming town of Ballard, California, had ever experienced.
It was also great publicity for the Hollywood newcomer, whose
private life was far more fascinating than her acting career.
The notorious gossip surrounding her two subsequent marriages
(to bandleader Artie Shaw and singer-superstar Frank Sinatra)
and romance with Howard Hughes eventually forced Gardner into
self-imposed exile in Europe, where she surrounded herself until
her death with a bevy of admiring playboys and celebrated matadors.*

Joan Crawford and Alfred Steele, 1955

*The former shop girl, jazz-baby flapper, queen of MGM,
and Hollywood's most durable star reinvented herself one last time
when she married Pepsi-Cola chairman Al Steele in a small
penthouse ceremony at the Flamingo Hotel in Las Vegas.
When he died four years later, the broken-hearted one-time wife
of Douglas Fairbanks, Jr., Franchot Tone, and Philip Terry
continued acting when she could and circling the globe in behalf of
her adopted company, manically installing soft-drink dispensers
on the sets of all of her subsequent films.*

Esther Williams and Lucille Ball (with Van Johnson)
EASY TO WED, 1946
Playing hard-to-get in this light remake of Libelled Lady,
boyishly handsome Johnson doesn't stand a chance with body-beautiful
Williams and red-headed Ball both vying for his attentions.
Although the ditsy former Goldwyn Girl eventually loses the
on-screen marriage game to MGM's favorite bathing beauty,
Ball and off-screen hubby Desi Arnaz would score big a few years
later with the premiere of their timeless I Love Lucy *television series*

Maureen O'Hara (with John Wayne and Charles Fitzsimons)
THE QUIET MAN, 1952

*Although the true-grit star of over 150 Hollywood actioners preferred
Latin women in real life (his three wives were all South American
beauties), Wayne as the ex-prizefighter who returns to his Irish roots
in this John Ford-directed masterpiece falls madly in love and marries
a local flame-headed beauty, played by Dublin-born O'Hara.*

*As full of Irish nonsense as the Blarney Stone itself, the
Oscar-winning crowd pleaser also packs a surprising sexual punch;
the morning after the nuptials, a neighbor spies the broken wedding
bed and bellows the memorable line, "Impetuous! Homeric!"*

Debbie Reynolds and Eddie Fisher, 1955

*When America's favorite sweetheart and teen-idol crooner cut the
cake after their three-minute civil ceremony in upstate New York,
the union was labeled "perfect" by fan magazines around the country.
Stabbed in the back four years later when her best friend,
Elizabeth Taylor, snatched Fisher away, the former Miss Burbank
rode a wave of fan sympathy that ironically pushed her popularity
to a peak. The "unsinkable Debbie Reynolds" continued on long
after her ex-husband's career (and marriage to Taylor) had failed,
eventually marrying the wealthy owner of a chain of shoe stores
and taking her song-and-dance act on the road.*

Elizabeth Taylor and Eddie Fisher, 1959

*Having already converted to Judaism for her previous marriage,
the lovely twenty-seven-year-old former wife of Nicky Hilton
and Michael Wilding and widow of showman Mike Todd married
Fisher, her last wedding's best man, outraging fans by breaking up
the singer's marriage to America's sweetheart, Debbie Reynolds.
Recovering the public's sympathy only after a near-death episode,
Hollywood's last true love goddess and sometime-homewrecker
next commenced her ten-year stop-start love-in with*
Cleopatra *costar Richard Burton.*

Natalie Wood and Robert Wagner, 1957

A perfect love match by all accounts, the handsome bobby-sox idol
and former child star-turned-leading lady enjoyed a long stretch of
wedded bliss (at least by Hollywood standards), before another teen
idol named Warren Beatty wooed Wood away. Divorced in 1963,
the former couple remarried, Taylor-Burton-style, nine years later.
Soon after Wood drowned tragically in 1981, Wagner, the star
of the hit TV series "Hart to Hart," married his costar in the
1967 sex-scandal flick Banning, *red-headed '60s starlet*
and woman-about-town Jill St. John.

Barbara Stanwyck (with Burt Lancaster)

SORRY, WRONG NUMBER, 1948

*It's hard to believe the neurotic, bed-ridden character in this film-noir
adaptation of the famous 1943 radio play could once have been a
beautiful bride. With Stanwyck bedecked in a sumptuous Edith Head-
designed gown and just married to one of Hollywood's handsomest
young actors, this scene looks more like a Tinseltown publicity shot
for a glamorous real-life wedding than a prelude to murder.*

Elizabeth Taylor and Nicky Hilton, 1950

*When hotel heir and playboy Conrad Nicholson Hilton, Jr.
(known as "Nicky") married the fetching seventeen-year-old MGM
star in a lavish Beverly Hills wedding, there were as many paparazzi
attending the ceremony as invited guests. More a studio-staged event
to publicize the actress's upcoming role in* Father of the Bride,
*the ill-fated union lasted as long as the couple's three-month
European honeymoon (irreconcilable differences were cited in
divorce court), shorter even than Conrad Sr.'s brief run
with another much-married MGM starlet, Zsa Zsa Gabor.*

Priscilla and Elvis Presley, 1967

A southern gentleman at heart, The King had courted his striking future wife for seven years (under the watchful eye of her army-general dad) before they finally tied the knot at a glitzed-out late-Elvis-style Las Vegas ceremony. Only sixteen when she first met the pelvis-swinging singer, the former Priscilla Beaulieu kept the beat alive in their stormy marriage for six years, eventually fleeing the Memphis-mafia-induced madness of Graceland. When the superstar died in 1977 at the age of 42, his ex-wife-turned-actress gladly reemerged as the Widow Presley, overseeing a multimillion-dollar empire in the name of their only daughter, Lisa-Marie.

47

Lucille Ball (with Desi Arnaz)

THE LONG, LONG TRAILER, 1954 (ABOVE)

*America's best-loved TV couple had already been married for
fourteen years when they starred as newlyweds in this
Vincente Minelli-directed comedy that played on the antics of their
hit television series. Six years Arnaz's senior and already forty-three
years old as the blushing bride in* The Long, Long Trailer, *
the redhead and former MGM chorus girl had first met her Cuban,
bongo-playing future husband on the set of the latter's
1940 RKO screen debut in* Too Many Girls.

Raquel Welch and Patrick Curtis, 1967 (right)

*Forming a business partnership with husband-to-be Curtis in
the mid-'60s to promote her fledgling acting career, the one-time
beauty contestant and cocktail waitress became an overnight
sex symbol without ever having appeared in a single important film.
Her career ignited, the former Raquel Tejada eventually married
her press-agent Svengali, only to dump him a few years
later after her position as an international star and
reigning sex goddess was firmly established.*

Frank Sinatra and Ava Gardner, 1951 (above)
and Mia Farrow, 1966 (right)

Singer, actor, radio and TV star, movie producer, and wealthy businessman, the former teen-idol bobby soxer is as famous for his associations with the world's most glamorous women as he is for his show-biz Chairman of the Board status. After divorcing his Italian sweetheart first wife Nancy, Sinatra began a whirlwind romantic roadshow that included a tempestuous relationship and marriage to Hollywood siren Ava Gardner (they divorced after six years) and a two-year union with fey actress and sometime flower child Mia Farrow (with an ill-fated fling with Lauren Bacall in-between). In the 1970s, Old Blue Eyes finally "retired" to Palm Springs with his last and present wife, Barbara, a former Las Vegas showgirl and the widow of Zeppo Marx.

Diana Rigg (with George Lazenby)

On Her Majesty's Secret Service, 1969 (above)

The sixth opus of the popular James Bond series featured no Sean Connery, who turned down the role before the producers had found a replacement in Roger Moore. But at least audiences finally got to see a more human side of Agent 007, who married Rigg and seemed poised to finally live happily ever after. Unfortunately, this installment of the adventure epic also featured the series' only tragic ending.

Jayne Mansfield and Mickey Hargitay, 1958 (right)

The voluptuous sexpot actress of whom Bette Davis once remarked, "Dramatic art in her opinion is knowing how to fill a sweater," was one of the more famous Marilyn Monroe clones to arise in the 1950s. The smarter-than-she-looked starlet consolidated her sex-kitten image by marrying bodybuilder Hargitay at the peak of her popularity. When the public soon tired of the self-promoting star of The Girl Can't Help It *and* Will Success Spoil Rock Hunter?, *Mansfield appeared with her husband in a string of low-budget European productions before her death in a car accident in 1967.*

Elizabeth Taylor and Michael Wilding, 1952

*Catching her breath after a whirlwind first marriage to
Nicky Hilton, the nineteen-year-old English-born beauty continued
her record-breaking march down the aisle with the first of her
two British husbands (Richard Burton was the other), wedding the
much-older patrician star of 1940s films in a fifteen-minute civil
ceremony in London. Wilding's fifteen minutes of fame as Mr. Liz
Taylor actually stretched into five years before the love-fickle actress
dumped him to marry showman Mike Todd in 1957.*

Rita Hayworth and Aly Khan, 1949

The leading love goddess of the 1940s, Hayworth once remarked:
"I haven't had everything from life. I've had too much."
And famous husbands were no exception. Married five times,
the ex-Mrs. Orson Welles landed her most celebrated catch when she
met the fabulously wealthy Muslim spiritual leader-cum-playboy son
of the Aga Khan while touring Europe on a movie publicity tour.
After their transatlantic tryst caused a worldwide scandal
(the Aly Khan was not yet divorced from his first wife), the movie star
and her prince married quietly in the south of France.
Eventually discovering that the Riviera high-life was no
fairy tale after all, Hayworth left her husband two years later
and returned to Hollywood.

Delores Costello and John Barrymore, 1928

*Hollywood's silent-screen swells turned out en masse when the
attractive blonde actress and daughter of celebrated stage actor-
turned-screen star Maurice Costello married the scion of America's
foremost acting clan in a lavish, Gatsby-style Beverly Hills wedding.
Having met when the Great Profile handpicked his future wife
to be his costar in the Warner Bros. smash* The Sea Beast,
*the couple eventually divorced, but not before starting their own
acting dynasty. Their son, John Drew Barrymore, enjoyed some
popularity as an actor in the '50s, and <u>his</u> daughter, Drew,
made an auspicious screen debut as the six-year-old who befriends
the space invader in* E.T.—The Extra-Terrestrial.

Joanne Woodward and Paul Newman, 1958

Wed in a quickie Las Vegas ceremony at the Hotel El Rancho Vegas, the Oscar-winning superstar duo have far outlasted the quickie Vegas-style marriages of most of their peers. Appearing in a number of pictures together (Newman has also directed his wife in a few films, including the well-received Rachel, Rachel*), the publicity-shy Connecticut couple was once asked to divulge the secret of their long relationship. When Newman answered definitively, "Respect," Woodward was quick to add, "And humor!"*

Janet Leigh and Tony Curtis, 1951

*A personal discovery of aging movie legend Norma Shearer,
the sweet-faced College of the Pacific music major with no acting
experience became an overnight celebrity when she married the former
Bernie Schwartz, Universal Studios' popular pin-up boy and latest
swashbuckling hero (with a Bronx accent!). As both their careers took
off throughout the '50s, the duo became one of Hollywood's best-loved
couples. Interestingly, when their marriage ultimately failed and the
two divorced in 1962, Leigh's star (it had burned brightest two years
earlier in* Psycho*) gradually dimmed, while her ex-husband continued
to enjoy some success in light comedies throughout the '60s.*

Marilyn Monroe and Joe DiMaggio, 1954

*The storybook wedding of the curvaceous blonde with the sexy wiggle
and husky voice and the retired New York Yankees superstar capped
off a year in which Monroe had become Twentieth Century-Fox's
biggest box-office draw* (Gentlemen Prefer Blondes, How To
Marry a Millionaire). *Incensed by the publicity surrounding the
star's next picture,* The Seven Year Itch *(remember the scene with
the subway grating), DiMaggio tried unsuccessfully to reel in his sex
goddess wife, but the marriage ended nine months after it had begun.
Monroe's third and last marriage, to playwright Arthur Miller
("Egghead Weds Hourglass") lasted longer, ending only after the
media-hounded, misunderstood "broad with her future behind her"
began losing her lifelong battle against drug addiction and depression.*

Orson Welles and Ruth Warrick
CITIZEN KANE, 1941 (ABOVE)
Irving Thalberg and Norma Shearer, 1927 (right)

Characters in real life and <u>reel</u> life, moguls have always fascinated Hollywood.
After true-life MGM production chief Thalberg married silent-screen star
Norma Shearer in a much-ballyhooed Tinseltown wedding (the actress soon
reigned as the First Lady of Metro), he consolidated his position in much
the same way as the title character of Orson Welles's cinematic masterpiece.
Later, the vicissitudes of studio politics and bad health ended the hard-working
movie mogul's hegemony at MGM almost as quickly as it had begun
(he was replaced by David Selznick). His brief reign in Xanadu over,
the man who almost single-handedly created the world's greatest movie studio
died a broken man at the age of thirty-seven.

Elizabeth Taylor and Richard Burton, 1964 (right)

THE TAMING OF THE SHREW, 1967 (OVERLEAF)

The most infamous lovers in the world (both on-screen and off) became the most
celebrated newlyweds in the world when they divorced their respective spouses
and married a year after falling in love on the set of the big-budget disaster
Cleopatra. *(During the wedding ceremony, the bride and groom treated guests*
to a one-performance-only poetry reading of "World Enough and Time.")
Eventually known simply as "Liz and Dick," the media-hounded couple
became more famous for Taylor's jewels and their public brawls than for any of
their mostly mediocre movie collaborations (the exceptions were films such as
Who's Afraid of Virginia Woolf? *and* The Taming of the Shrew
that seemed in part to mirror the couple's tempestuous real-life relationship).
The Burtons eventually divorced in the early '70s, only to remarry in 1975
in a mud-walled African village and then redivorce the following year.

Michelle Pfeiffer (with Al Pacino)
SCARFACE, 1983 (RIGHT)
Talia Shire (with Gianni Russo)
THE GODFATHER, 1972 (OVERLEAF)
*The lavishly-staged weddings in Francis Ford Coppola's and
Brian dePalma's cinematic gangster masterpieces add a decidedly
human touch to two of the grimmest epics ever committed to celluloid.
When Shire, as the Godfather's daughter, marries a bookie in her
father's fiefdom, we are introduced to the somehow touching familial
matrix that underpins and propels a larger family of Mafia
chieftains and street thugs. Also touching, the wedding of up-and-
coming drug lord Tony and cocaine-addicted Elvira in* Scarface
*is a happy moment in an ultimately doomed union, a metaphor
for lust and greed and the dark side of the American way.*

Yvette Mimieux (with George Hamilton)

THE LIGHT IN THE PIAZZA, 1962

*Beautiful 1960s starlet Yvette Mimieux makes
an unusual bride playing the retarded daughter of
Olivia de Havilland in this quirky but touching
MGM love story-cum-travelogue, filmed in Florence
and based on the novel by Elizabeth Spencer.
When de Havilland eventually falls for pretty-boy
Hamilton's father, played by Rossano Brazzi,
the hankie-wringing soaper offers a double dose of
star-studded romance and a classic Hollywood ending.*

Maria Shriver and Arnold Schwarzenegger, 1986

*When the Austrian policeman's son and former Mr. Olympia
wedded JFK's niece in St. Francis Xavier Church in Hyannisport,
everyone from the groom's* Conan the Barbarian *costar Grace Jones
(in full-length fur and sunglasses) to Andy Warhol and
Jacqueline Onassis attended the Fellini-esque media event.
Although Kennedys had long had ties to Tinseltown (grandfather
Joe had been in the movie business, and Shriver's aunt had been
married to actor Peter Lawford), the marriage of America's biggest
movie star and muscle-flexing arch-conservative to the petite
broadcast journalist and left-wing Democrat was one of
the decade's (and Hollywood's) unlikeliest unions.*

Katharine Ross (with Dustin Hoffman)
THE GRADUATE, 1967

A heroic act of defiance by two young people whose destinies were being manipulated by an older generation, the final sequence in this lushly-filmed, Mike Nichols-directed box-office smash influenced generation-gap moviegoers around the world and remains one of the most famous (and infamous!) wedding scenes in movie history. The film also made the Oscar-nominated Hoffman and Ross as the star-crossed lovers overnight sensations.

CREDITS AND SOURCES

TEXT: J. SPENCER BECK

DESIGN: LISA LYTTON-SMITH
PICTURE EDITOR: LESLIE FRATKIN

Front Cover: Photofest
3: Courtesy The Kobal Collection
7: Courtesy The Kobal Collection
8: Neal Peters Collection
9: Photofest
10: Photofest
11: Photofest
12: Everett Collection
13: Photofest
14: Photofest
16: Lester Glassner Collection/Neal Peters
17: Photofest
19: Photofest
21: Culver Pictures
22: Photofest
23: Courtesy The Kobal Collection
25: Neal Peters Collection
26: Courtesy The Kobal Collection
27: Neal Peters Collection
29: Everett Collection
30: Photofest
31: UPI/Bettmann
32: AP/Wide World Photos
33: Neal Peters Collection
35: Photofest
37: Courtesy The Kobal Collection
39: Photofest
41: Globe Photos
42: Everett Collection
43: Photofest
45: UPI/Bettmann
46-47: Neal Peters Collection
48: Lester Glassner Collection/Neal Peters
49: Neal Peters Collection
50: Lester Glassner Collection/Neal Peters
51: Globe Photos
52: Everett Collection
53: UPI/Bettmann
55: UPI/Bettmann
57: Neal Peters Collection
59: Photofest
60: Photofest
61: Photofest
63: UPI/Bettmann
64: Courtesy The Kobal Collection
65: Everett Collection
67: Archive Photos
68-69: Courtesy The Kobal Collection
71: Neal Peters Collection
72-73: Culver Pictures
74-75: Culver Pictures
77: UPI/Bettmann
78: Culver Pictures
Back Cover: Photofest